CHICAGO
BULLS

by Brian Howell

Published by ABDO Publishing Company, 8000 West 78th Street, Edina, Minnesota 55439. Copyright © 2012 by Abdo Consulting Group, Inc. International copyrights reserved in all countries. No part of this book may be reproduced in any form without written permission from the publisher. SportsZone™ is a trademark and logo of ABDO Publishing Company.

Printed in the United States of America,
North Mankato, Minnesota
062011
092011

 THIS BOOK CONTAINS AT LEAST 10% RECYCLED MATERIALS.

Editor: Seth Putnam
Copy Editor: Anna Comstock
Series design and cover production: Christa Schneider
Interior production: Carol Castro

Photo Credits: Amy Sancetta/AP Images, cover; Mark J. Terrill/AP Images, 1; Michael S. Green/AP Images, 4, 44; Jack Smith/AP Images, 7, 43 (middle); Michael Conroy/AP Images, 8; William Straeter/AP Images, 10; AP Photo/AP Images, 13, 15, 16; John Swart/AP Images, 18, 29, 42 (top and bottom); Ron Frehm/AP Images, 21, 25, 32, 42 (middle), 43 (top); Craig Fujii/AP Images, 22; Beth A. Keiser/AP Images, 26; Bill Kostroun/AP Images, 31; Frank Franklin II/AP Images, 34, 43 (bottom); Jeff Roberson/AP Images, 37; Stephen J. Carrera/AP Images, 38; Chris Young/AP Images, 41; Mike Fisher/AP Images, 47

Library of Congress Cataloging-in-Publication Data
Howell, Brian, 1974-
  Chicago Bulls / by Brian Howell.
     p. cm. -- (Inside the NBA)
  Includes index.
  ISBN 978-1-61783-152-2
  1. Chicago Bulls (Basketball team)--History--Juvenile literature. I. Title.
  GV885.52.C45H68 2012
  796.323'6477311--dc22
                            2011013803

TABLE OF CONTENTS

CHAPTER 1

END OF AN ERA

T he Utah Jazz's last-second shot hit off the rim and bounced away from the hoop. The clock went to zero, the buzzer sounded, and the Chicago Bulls were the National Basketball Association (NBA) champions for the sixth time in only eight years.

Chicago's superstar guard Michael Jordan leaped in the air and pumped his fist. Moments later, he found Bulls head coach Phil Jackson in the middle of the court, and the two men gave each other a hug.

"That was beautiful," Jackson told Jordan as they embraced. "What a finish!" What a finish, indeed.

That game was played on June 14, 1998. Going into it, the Bulls led the Jazz three games to two in the NBA Finals. The first team to four wins would be the league champion. Getting that fourth win was not easy

The Bulls' Scottie Pippen, *left*, drives to the basket against the Utah Jazz's Jeff Hornacek in Game 4 of the 1998 NBA Finals.

for the Bulls, because they were playing on Utah's home court at the Delta Center in Salt Lake City.

In the closing seconds, Utah led 86–85. Chicago, however, had Jordan on the court. Many consider Jordan to be the greatest basketball player in history. And he was determined to win that game. Jordan stole the ball from Utah's All-Star forward Karl Malone. As the clock ticked down, he prepared for his final shot. Utah's Bryon Russell guarded him. Jordan faked a move to the right. That got Russell off balance. Jordan took advantage and launched a 17-foot jump shot. It went in with 5.2 seconds left. The Bulls now had an 87–86 lead. When Utah's final shot bounced off the rim, that was where the score stayed.

"It was a do-or-die situation. I let the time tick to where I had the court right where I wanted it to be," Jordan said after the game. "As soon as Russell reached, he gave me a clear lane. I stopped, pulled up, and had an easy jump shot. Great look, and it went in."

The win in Utah gave the Bulls the 1998 NBA championship. It was not just the end to a great season for the Bulls, however. It was the end of a great era of success.

In eight seasons from 1991 to 1998, the Bulls won six NBA championships. During that time, Jackson was the coach,

The Bulls' Michael Jordan, *left*, holds the MVP trophy as coach Phil Jackson holds the NBA championship trophy after the Bulls won the 1998 NBA Finals.

while Jordan and Scottie Pippen were the star players. Only two teams in NBA history have won more than Chicago's six championships, the Boston Celtics and the Los Angeles Lakers. The Celtics are the only other team to win six titles in an eight-year span.

Leaving the Door Open

On January 13, 1999, Michael Jordan announced his retirement from the NBA. That day, he said he was "99.9 percent" sure he was done playing. Well, that 0.1 percent got the best of him a few years later. In 2001, he signed with the Washington Wizards. Jordan played two more seasons before retiring for good.

Cameras flash as the Chicago Bulls are introduced before Game 5 of the NBA Finals against the Utah Jazz on June 12, 1998, in Chicago.

As the Bulls went through the 1997–98 season, there was speculation that it would be the last year for Jordan, Pippen, and Jackson together. The contracts for all three of them expired after the 1998 NBA Finals. And even as the Bulls celebrated their championship in Salt Lake City, Pippen knew the end had probably come.

"I think this is probably it. It's pretty much over," Pippen said after the 1998 Finals win. Unfortunately for Bulls fans, Pippen was right. Jordan retired and Pippen went to the Houston Rockets. Jackson sat out a year before moving to Los Angeles to coach the Lakers.

Jordan was Chicago's main star. In fact, he was the biggest

star in the NBA. When he retired after the 1998 season, he was still one of the best players in the league.

"My physical skills are as strong as ever," he said during his retirement speech on January 13, 1999. "I promised myself that when the mental challenge began to fade I would leave. That time is now here. I know from a career standpoint I have accomplished everything I could as an individual."

During their time together, the Chicago Bulls were one of the greatest teams in NBA history. The Celtics and the Lakers have won more championships, but for most of the 1990s, it was the Bulls who dominated the league.

At the end of Game 6 in Salt Lake City, NBA commissioner David Stern presented the Bulls with the championship trophy. As he did so, he

Where Did They Go?

The 1998 Bulls team was full of stars. But all of them were gone before the 1998–99 season. Michael Jordan retired. Scottie Pippen was traded to the Houston Rockets. After playing one season in Houston, he played four years for the Portland Trail Blazers. Pippen then finished his career with 23 games with the Bulls in 2003–04. Bulls forward Dennis Rodman left the team before the 1999–2000 season, too. He played one season with the Los Angeles Lakers and one with the Dallas Mavericks. As for coach Phil Jackson, he became coach of the Lakers. In 2010, he led the Lakers to their fifth NBA title in his 10 seasons as their coach.

said, "To the Chicago Bulls, the 1998 NBA champion and a team for the ages, congratulations."

With six titles in eight years, led by Jordan, Pippen, and Jackson, the Bulls were a far cry from their humble beginnings.

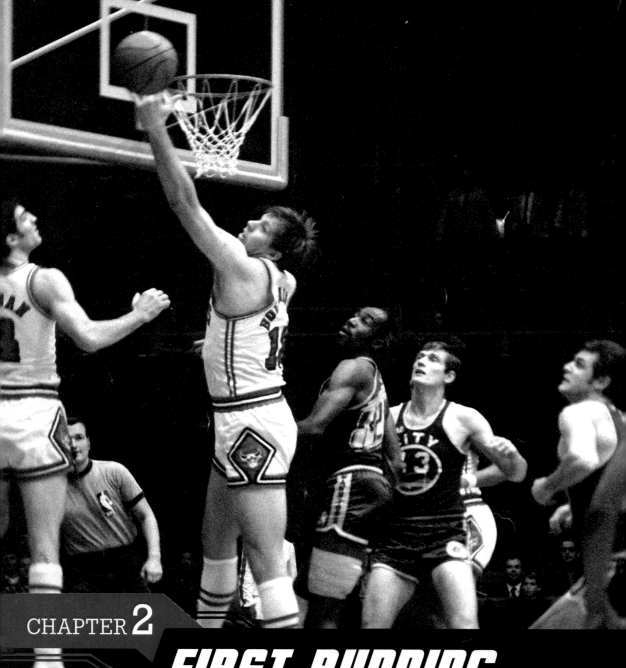

CHAPTER 2

FIRST RUNNING OF THE BULLS

Others had tried and failed to have a successful professional basketball team in Chicago. But in 1966, Dick Klein was determined to make it work. He was the leader of a group of five men who owned the newest team in the NBA: the Chicago Bulls.

"The game never was properly exploited in Chicago," Klein said of previous failed attempts. "It'll take a couple of years to break even financially, but with proper promotion, I'm sure we'll make money eventually."

The Bulls, who became the NBA's 10th team, were destined to struggle. At least that was what most people thought. The Bulls were allowed to pick two players from each of the other nine NBA teams. But each of those teams could protect seven players on their rosters. That meant the Bulls would not be able to get any of the league's best players. The Bulls were also forced to pick at the

Tom Boerwinkle of the Chicago Bulls deflects a rebound to teammate Jerry Sloan (4) in an NBA game with the San Francisco Warriors on December 11, 1969.

bottom of the college draft. That meant they would not have a shot to take University of Michigan star Cazzie Russell. The Bulls had been hoping to get Russell, since he was a Chicago native.

Chicago fans did not expect much of the Bulls. Only about 350 season tickets were sold for the 11,002-seat arena for that first season. But despite what some people thought of the Bulls, Klein was excited. He could not wait for the Bulls to get on the court. "I want a Chicago Bull to be a cross between a tiger and a water buffalo," he said.

In that first season, the Bulls did not dominate. They did not even have a winning record. But they were much better than expected. They finished 33–48 and qualified for the playoffs. Led by Guy Rodgers, Bob Boozer, and Jerry Sloan, the Bulls surprised the league with their speed and good defense, but were eliminated in the first round.

Coach Johnny "Red" Kerr led the Bulls to their second playoffs in two seasons, but he left the team after they were eliminated again in the first round. He was replaced by Dick Motta, who was hired away from Weber State College in Utah.

Chet Walker, *right*, of the Chicago Bulls has his eye on a loose ball as the Los Angeles Lakers' Gail Goodrich, *center*, struggles to capture it.

Motta came to the Bulls as a young and inexperienced coach for the 1968–69 season. He was just 37 years old and had never coached professional basketball. He was not worried

Better than the Rest

In their first NBA season, the Bulls went 33–48. Through 2010–11, no expansion team in NBA history has ever won more games than the Bulls did in their first season.

went 51–31 in the 1970–71 season, the first time they had ever posted a winning record.

In 1973–74, the Bulls defeated the Detroit Pistons in the first round of the playoffs. It was the first playoff series win in Bulls history. That win got them to the Western Conference finals, where they lost to the Milwaukee Bucks. The next year they got back to the conference finals, but there they lost to the Golden State Warriors.

Motta was not the only reason the Bulls had a winning record. They had players with great talent, too. Bob Love was a three-time All-Star for the Bulls for nine years, from 1968 to 1977. The 6-foot-8 forward led the team in scoring seven years in a row. As of the 2010–11 season, he was the third-highest scorer in team history, behind only Michael Jordan and Scottie Pippen.

about it, though. "It isn't that awfully hard in this league," he said. "It isn't that different. We don't have the best club, but I'll be okay."

And Motta was okay. In his first year, the Bulls failed to make the playoffs. But it was Motta who became the first coach to make the team a winner. He coached the Bulls for eight seasons, leading them to the playoffs six times. They

Bob Love receives the game ball in Chicago on January 25, 1974, after he scores his 10,000th point during a game against the Seattle SuperSonics.

Jerry Sloan was a guard for the Bulls from the team's beginning in 1966. He was an All-Star twice. Through 2010–11, he ranked fourth all-time in scoring. He later became the Bulls coach for two-and-a-half seasons before resigning mid-year and eventually coaching the Utah Jazz for more than 22 seasons. In addition to Love and Sloan, the early Bulls had Chet "The Jet" Walker, Norm Van Lier, and Tom Boerwinkle.

A talented forward, Love averaged 20.6 points per game in nine seasons in Chicago. Van Lier was a three-time All-Star

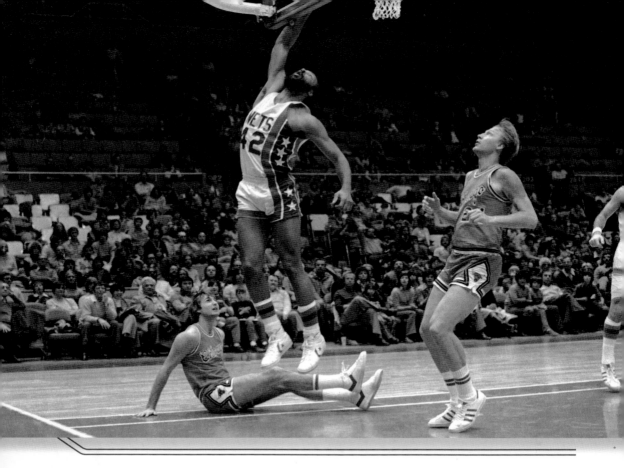

The Chicago Bulls' John Laskowski has the best seat in the house to watch the New York Nets' Mel Davis score in a game in 1977.

with the Bulls. And while Boerwinkle was never an All-Star and he did not score much, he was a great rebounder. He tallied 5,745 by the end of his career. Michael Jordan is the only player in team history to snag more rebounds than Boerwinkle through 2010–11.

Motta's final season in Chicago, 1975–76, was a disaster. Injuries and other problems led the Bulls to the worst record in the NBA at 24–58. Motta left after that season.

During the next eight seasons, the Bulls struggled. They made the playoffs just two times during those years. Eight different men served as head coach, including Sloan.

Artis Gilmore, a 7-foot-2 center, and Reggie Theus, a 6-foot-7 guard, were All-Stars for Chicago in those years. But they never could guide the Bulls to a championship. Gilmore and Theus played four seasons together. The best of those years was 1980–81. Both Gilmore and Theus were All-Stars, and they led the Bulls to a 45–37 record. But after beating the New York Knicks in the first round of the playoffs, the Bulls were eliminated by the Boston Celtics in the second round.

Their time together was short. In the summer of 1982, the Bulls traded Gilmore to the San Antonio Spurs. And in February of 1984, they traded Theus to the Kansas City Kings.

At the end of the 1983–84 season, the Bulls had just 27

He Was a Winner

Dick Motta had a 356–300 record as the Bulls' coach from 1968 to 1976. Through 2010–11, only Phil Jackson has won more games in Chicago (545–193). Motta led the Bulls to four straight 50-win seasons and was named NBA Coach of the Year in 1971. He later coached the Washington Bullets, the Dallas Mavericks, the Sacramento Kings, and the Denver Nuggets. His 935 victories rank 11th all-time in NBA history through 2010–11. And Motta led the Bullets to the 1978 NBA championship.

wins. Only the Indiana Pacers, with 26 wins, were worse that season. During the last 15 games of that season, the Bulls went 1–14. Frustrated fans began staying away from Chicago Stadium. The Bulls were in desperate need of a change— and a little luck.

The Bulls got both on June 19, 1984, two months after their horrible season ended.

CHAPTER 3

"AIR JORDAN" ARRIVES

The 1984 NBA Draft was held in New York on June 19. Every year, the draft allows NBA teams to pick from the best amateur players.

Most people could guess the order of the first three overall picks. They expected the Houston Rockets to use the first pick on Hakeem Olajuwon, a 7-foot center from the University of Houston. A lot of people guessed the Portland Trail Blazers would then take Sam Bowie, a 7-foot-1 center from the University of Kentucky.

That left the Bulls with the number three pick. A young man named Michael Jordan had been making big splashes at the University of North Carolina. He was the national College Player of the Year in 1984. He would also help the United States win a gold medal that year at the Olympic Games in Los Angeles. In 1984,

Michael Jordan dunks during the slam-dunk competition of the 1988 NBA All-Star weekend. Jordan was inducted into the Hall of Fame in 2009.

PATH TO STARDOM

Michael Jordan was cut from his varsity basketball team as a high school sophomore. But by the time he was a senior, he was a McDonald's All-American. He then earned a basketball scholarship to the University of North Carolina (UNC). As a freshman at UNC, he hit the game-winning shot in the national championship game. He was the Atlantic Coast Conference Freshman of the Year in 1982. He was also an All-American in 1983 and 1984. In 1984, he was named the College Player of the Year.

Jordan provided fans with a lot of highlights throughout his career. One of his most memorable games came in 1986. In Game 2 of the playoffs against the Boston Celtics, Jordan scored an NBA-playoff-record 63 points. The Bulls still lost to the Celtics, 135–131 in double-overtime. The Bulls lost all three games of that series, but Jordan shined, averaging 43.7 points per game.

professional players could not be on the U.S. Olympic basketball teams.

The Bulls wanted Jordan. "Unless Portland pulls a big surprise and takes Jordan, we'll take him," said Rod Thorn, who was the Bulls' general manager. "If they take Jordan, we take Sam Bowie."

Luckily for the Bulls, Houston did take Olajuwon, and Portland did take Bowie. Olajuwon wound up having a Hall of Fame career and is considered one of the greatest centers ever. Bowie, on the other hand, turned into an average player who never made an All-Star team. The Bulls got Jordan.

Fans cheered his selection. The Bulls were thrilled, too. But Jordan? He just wanted to play. "I haven't met Coach [Kevin] Loughery yet, but I'm looking forward to

Michael Jordan, *right*, shields the ball against the New York Knicks in 1996. He became known for sticking out his tongue during intense play.

playing for him," Jordan said on draft night. "I don't know about turning a team around. I'm just looking forward to playing and contributing what I can."

While everyone in Chicago was excited for Jordan's arrival, nobody could have predicted how great he would become.

From the start, Jordan made his mark on the Bulls.

They won just 27 games the year before he arrived. They quickly improved to 38 wins in

Wrong Foot Forward

Michael Jordan suffered just one major injury during his NBA career. He broke his foot in the third game of his second season. He missed 64 games because of the injury. But he returned in time to help the Bulls get to the playoffs.

The Los Angeles Lakers' Vlade Divac, *right*, reaches for a steal from the Bulls' Scottie Pippen, *left*, in Game 3 of the NBA Finals on June 7, 1991.

his first year, and they made the playoffs every year of his career with the Bulls.

Jordan was known for sticking out his tongue when he played. He was also known for his high-flying style that earned him the nickname "Air Jordan." It did not take long for Jordan to prove he was a great player. He dazzled the Chicago crowd in his first game by scoring 16 points and dishing out seven assists in a win over the Washington Bullets.

"We're a different team with Jordan," Loughery said that night. Jordan's teammates were impressed, too. "We're all better with him out there," teammate Orlando Woolridge said. His opponents were in

Pippen, a Star

Scottie Pippen came from a little-known college: the University of Central Arkansas. Nevertheless, there were high hopes for his professional career. The Seattle SuperSonics drafted Pippen with the fifth overall pick in the 1987 NBA Draft. Chicago immediately pulled off a trade for him. That gave Bulls star Michael Jordan the high-quality player he needed by his side. In 11 seasons with the Bulls from 1987 to 1998, Pippen made the All-Star team seven times. He was also on the All-Defensive first team seven times in those seasons. Pippen helped the Bulls win six NBA championships. In 2010, he was inducted into the Basketball Hall of Fame.

awe. "He is one of a kind," said Washington's Dudley Bradley, who guarded Jordan that first night.

As a rookie in 1984–85, Jordan averaged 28.2 points per game. That ranked him third in the entire NBA. No player in Bulls history had ever scored that much. Jordan also showed off his all-around talent by averaging 6.5 rebounds and 5.9 assists per game.

That was just the beginning for Air Jordan, however. He finished his career with 32,292 points. Through 2010–11, that was the third-highest total in league history. In addition, Jordan led the league in scoring 10 times in his 13 years as a Bull. That included a remarkable 37.1 points per game during the 1986–87 season.

Jordan was much more than just a scorer, though. He was on the NBA's All-Defensive team nine times. He was Defensive Player of the Year in 1987–88. By the time he left the Bulls after the 1998 season, Jordan was considered by many to be the greatest player in NBA history. He was the league's MVP five times. He made the All-Star team 12 times. And he was MVP of the All-Star Game three times.

High-flying Jordan

Michael Jordan was a great all-around player. What dazzled fans the most, though, were his incredible leaping skills that led to amazing dunks. Jordan won the NBA's Slam Dunk Contest in both 1987 and 1988. In one of his most iconic moves, he would jump from the free-throw line and slam the ball through the net.

Most important to Jordan and Bulls fans, he led them to six NBA championships. Not surprisingly, he was named MVP of the Finals in all six of those championship runs. In 2009, Jordan was inducted into the Naismith Memorial Basketball Hall of Fame.

"[He was] simply the greatest to ever play the game of basketball," said John Paxson, who was Jordan's teammate for eight years. "He is the one player that each young person in this league should emulate and aspire to become. His work ethic, drive, skill level, and competitive spirit were unmatched."

The Bulls were one of the worst teams in the league when Michael Jordan arrived in 1984. By his fourth season, they were an elite team. They made the playoffs six times right before their championship successes. However, each time they were eliminated without making it out of the Eastern Conference. The problem was that the Bulls could not get past the Detroit Pistons. Detroit knocked Chicago out of the playoffs in 1988, 1989, and 1990. The Bulls just could not seem to find the right ingredients.

The Bulls would not win until they could unite great coaching with teachable players. They got both toward the end of the 1980s. Scottie Pippen was traded to the team shortly after being drafted by the Seattle SuperSonics in 1987.

Chicago Bulls coach Phil Jackson, *center*, argues with a referee after Scottie Pippen was ejected from a game on May 25, 1993.

Pippen, who had been a standout at the University of Central Arkansas, would pair with Jordan to create a lethal scoring tandem.

Then there was mastermind Phil Jackson. He took over as head coach in 1989 following an average playing career with the New York Knicks and the New Jersey Nets in the 1960s and 1970s. After just one season, Jackson put together the team that would win the Bulls' first championship. Under his guidance, the team would win three trophies in a row. That had not been done since the Boston Celtics dominated the Finals from 1959 to 1966.

CHAPTER 4

BEST TEAM EVER?

What Chicago did from 1990 to 1998 is perhaps second only to the Boston Celtics' run of 11 championships in 13 years. In eight seasons, coach Phil Jackson led the Bulls to six NBA titles. They won three in a row from 1991 to 1993, and another three in a row from 1996 to 1998.

"I think the '96 Bulls are the greatest of all time," Scottie Pippen said in a 2007 interview with NBA.com. "We had a dominant style, a dominant defense, and we were a very good offensive team. It was the way we dominated our opponents that separated ourselves."

The 1990–91 season started it all. Michael Jordan was the league's MVP. He and Pippen led the Bulls to a team-record 61 wins. In the Eastern Conference finals, the Bulls met up with their archrivals, the Detroit Pistons, who had knocked them out of the playoffs

Bulls coach Phil Jackson hugs Michael Jordan after the Bulls beat the Seattle SuperSonics 87–75 to win their fourth NBA championship.

in three previous seasons. This time, however, Jordan would not be denied. He led the Bulls to a four-game sweep of the Pistons. That sent the Bulls to the NBA Finals for the first time ever. In the Finals, Jordan averaged 31.2 points and 11.4 assists per game, leading the Bulls to a win against the Los Angeles Lakers.

"I'm numb," an emotional Jordan said after the championship-deciding Game 5 against Los Angeles. "I don't know what to do. I want to enjoy this; it's such a great feeling. When I came into this situation, we started from scratch. We started at the bottom and made it to the top. It's been a long, long seven years. A lot of bad teams, a lot of improvement. Step by step, inch by inch. I never gave up hope. I always had faith."

The next year the Bulls won a remarkable 67 games.

Global Star

Basketball made Michael Jordan famous. But what he did off the court made him the most recognizable athlete in the world. Jordan appeared in commercials for Nike, Coca Cola, Gatorade, McDonald's, and many other well-known products. Nike even created an "Air Jordan" shoe line that, through 2010–11, was still among the most popular basketball shoe choices for consumers. Jordan also starred in the popular movie Space Jam in 1996.

At the time, that was the fifth most in league history. They handily defeated Clyde Drexler and the Portland Trail Blazers in the Finals for another title. And the year after that, they made it a three in a row by beating Charles Barkley and the Phoenix Suns four games to two in the Finals.

The only thing that stopped the Bulls from a possible fourth championship was Jordan himself. After the team won the

Revelers take to the streets to celebrate the Bulls' win over the Portland Trail Blazers for the 1992 NBA championship.

1993 NBA title—its third in a row—Jordan surprised the basketball world by retiring. He was only 30 years old, but he said, "I just feel that I don't have anything else to prove." The next summer, he gave professional baseball a shot. He signed with the Chicago White Sox and played for their Double-A team, the Birmingham Barons. In 127 games, he hit .202 and stole 30 bases.

Jordan was gone from the Bulls for 21 months. He returned late in the 1994–95 season, but the Bulls were knocked out in the second round of the playoffs.

Horace Grant, the Bulls' bespectacled power forward, had proven to be a major rebounding force for the team during its previous championship run. When he left to go play for the Orlando Magic in

JACKSON'S IMPACT

Phil Jackson enjoyed a solid 12-year playing career with the New York Knicks and New Jersey Nets. That included winning an NBA title in 1973. However, Jackson really found his calling as a coach—few others have been at his level. Before the 1989–90 season, Jackson was named the Bulls' head coach. In nine seasons with the Bulls from 1989 to 1998, he led them to six championships. Chicago won at least 47 games in each of his seasons there.

Jackson then went on to coach the Los Angeles Lakers. In the 2009–10 season, the Lakers won their fifth title in 10 years with Jackson. By the time Jackson ended the 2010–11 season, he had won more rings than he had fingers to put them on. His 11 NBA titles as head coach were unmatched as of 2010–11. His record was 1,155–485 over his 20-year career. He was inducted into the Basketball Hall of Fame in 2007.

1994, the Bulls needed someone to fill his shoes. They traded for Dennis Rodman, who had been a part of the Pistons team that Chicago had a tough time beating years earlier. He was also the best rebounder in the NBA. He led the league in rebounding seven straight years from 1992 to 1998.

Rodman was a risk, however, because of his off-the-court behavior. Outside of basketball, he dealt with depression and a difficult family life. He was constantly in the media due to his bizarre fashion and strange antics. But it was a risk the Bulls were willing to take.

"We've just asked him to be focused on basketball when he steps on the court," Jordan said.

The risk paid off for Chicago. Rodman was one of

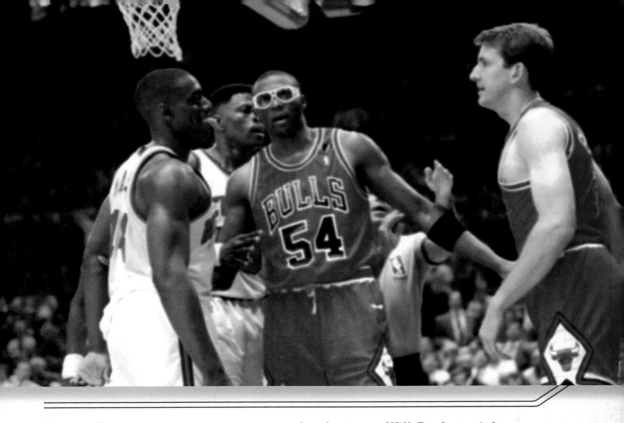

Horace Grant, *center*, acts as peacemaker between Will Perdue, *right*, and the New York Knicks' Anthony Mason during a game in 1992.

many Bulls players who thrived throughout the 1995–96 season. Jordan was once again the league MVP. He and Pippen were both first-team All-NBA performers that season. And Jordan, Pippen, and Rodman were first-team All-Defensive team selections. The Bulls had standout role players, too. Toni Kukoc, Luc Longley, Steve Kerr, and Ron Harper all offered significant support.

Those players and more combined to lead Chicago to a 72–10 record. They were the first, and as of 2011, the only team in NBA history to win 70 games in a season. Their dominance continued during the playoffs. The Bulls went 15–3 through the postseason. That

Chicago's Dennis Rodman pulls down a rebound in front of the Knicks' Charles Oakley, *left,* and Anthony Mason during a playoff game in 1996.

included a win over the Seattle SuperSonics in the NBA Finals. When it was all over, many recognized the 1995–96 Bulls as one of the best teams the NBA has ever seen.

At the very least, the Bulls had put themselves in the same class as the great Lakers and Celtics teams of the past. No team had won as many games in one season as the Bulls. Few teams had a collection of talent like Chicago. And they were not finished.

Chicago won 69 games during the 1996–97 season. With the same group of players, and Phil Jackson still as coach, the Bulls went 15–4 in the playoffs and beat the Utah Jazz in the NBA Finals.

Jackson, Jordan, Kukoc, Pippen, and Rodman all came back for one last hurrah in 1997–98. Pippen missed nearly half the season with an injury, but the Bulls still won 62 games. Jordan was once again the league's MVP. In the playoffs, the Bulls went 15–6 to again beat the Jazz in the Finals. They capped it off with Jordan's remarkable buzzer-beating shot to win Game 6.

When the season ended, there was little doubt about Chicago's greatness. Six championships in eight years is a remarkable feat. But when it was over in 1998, all of the Bulls' key components went their separate directions.

"Hopefully I've put enough memories out there," Jordan said. "I have another life, and I know I have to get to it at some point in time. Hopefully the fans can understand that."

By his second retirement, Jordan had been the Rookie of the Year. He won the league MVP Award five times. He was the playoff MVP six times. He made the All-Star team 14 times. And as of 2010–11, he was the third-highest scorer in league history, and he ranked second in career steals.

For the Bulls, the summer of 1998 was bittersweet. For the second time, they celebrated a third straight championship in June. But they spent the rest of the summer replacing Jordan, Pippen, Rodman, and Jackson.

Breaking the Record

In 1995–96, the Bulls set an NBA record with 72 regular-season wins. The previous record was 69 wins by the 1971–72 Los Angeles Lakers. The 1996–97 Bulls also won 69 games. As of 2010–11, the 72-win record still stood.

CHAPTER 5

THE NEW BULLS

In June of 1998, the Chicago Bulls were at the top of the basketball world. For a second time, they had won their third NBA championship in a row.

Before the next season began, though, the NBA went through a lockout. That meant the league prevented the players from playing because they could not agree on contract issues. The lockout lasted nearly seven months. When the NBA finally returned to action in February, the Bulls were a much different team.

Chicago was the defending champion, but stars Michael Jordan, Scottie Pippen, and Dennis Rodman were gone. Coach Phil Jackson had left the Bulls, too. Over were the glory days of the Bulls.

Tim Floyd took over as coach after Jackson left. And the role players that had helped Chicago win the title suddenly

Derrick Rose goes in for a dunk during a game against the New York Knicks in 2011. At the end of the regular season, Rose became the NBA's youngest MVP ever..

had to be the leaders. It was a formula that did not work. In one season, the Bulls went from being champion to being the worst team in the Eastern Conference.

Life would not get any easier for the Bulls for a while. In six seasons from 1998 to 2004, the Bulls were one of the worst teams in the NBA. They finished last in the Central Division in five of those six years. And they finished just sixth out of eight teams the other year.

There appeared to be a glimmer of hope at the end of the 2000–01 season. Elton Brand, who had been the number one choice in the 1999 NBA Draft, had become a star for the Bulls. In addition, forward Ron Mercer provided a good scoring punch. Forward Ron Artest, another 1999 first-round draft pick, was gaining a reputation for his great defense. And Brad Miller was developing into a solid young center.

Things were looking up, but that all changed in June 2001. On the night of the NBA Draft, the Bulls traded Brand to the Los Angeles Clippers for rookie forward Tyson Chandler. Then, in February 2002, the Bulls pulled off another trade. They sent their three best players, Artest, Mercer, and Miller, to the Indiana Pacers for Jalen Rose and others.

The trades were made in an effort to get better, but they did not work. Rose was on the

The Bulls' Tyson Chandler, *right*, and the Los Angeles Clippers' Elton Brand, *left*, get tangled up while fighting for a rebound in 2004.

downside of his career and played just one full season with the Bulls. Meanwhile, Chandler and center Eddy Curry developed slowly.

After years of trying, it was not until the 2004–05 season that the Bulls again found the right mix of talent. Directed by coach Scott Skiles, the Bulls went 47–35 and reached the playoffs for the first time since the championship season of 1998.

Curry had his best season as a Bull that year. He had help, too. Second-year point guard Kirk Hinrich had a great year. Rookies Ben Gordon, Luol Deng, and Andres Nocioni played well, too. For the first time since Jordan left, the Bulls

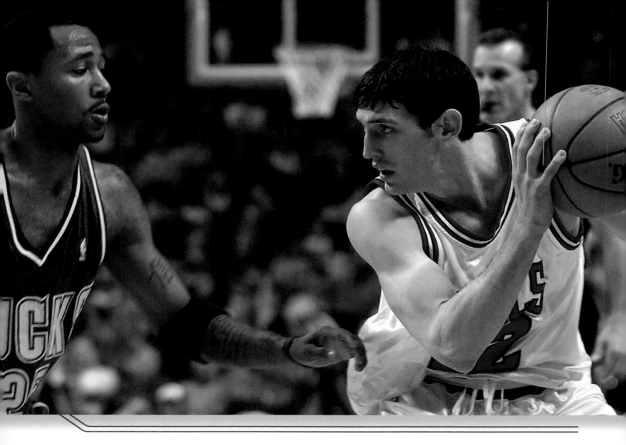

The Chicago Bulls' Kirk Hinrich, *right*, looks to drive against the Milwaukee Bucks' Maurice Williams, *left*, on March 7, 2005.

were a good team and had reason smile about the future.

"Everybody, including myself, is really excited," Hinrich said before the playoffs began. "We've been waiting for this a long time."

The Bulls lost in the first round against the Washington Wizards. Just getting back to the playoffs was a positive step for the Bulls, though. Curry was traded after the season. But Gordon, Deng, Hinrich, and Nocioni led the Bulls to the playoffs in 2006 and 2007, as well.

From 2005 to 2010, the Bulls made the playoffs five times in six years. Although the championship years were over, success had returned to Chicago basketball.

What the Bulls were missing was a star player. After missing the playoffs in 2007, the Bulls were hurting. They had a 1.7 percent chance of getting the number one pick in the NBA Draft the next year. But in the lottery to determine the selection order, they hit the jackpot and got it. They used that pick on University of Memphis point guard Derrick Rose.

Rose was the NBA's Rookie of the Year in 2008–09. The next year, he became an NBA All-Star. Although the Bulls lost to the Cleveland Cavaliers in the first round of the 2009 playoffs, things were looking up in Chicago. Rose quickly made a name for himself with his amazing crossover moves, his pinpoint passing, his deadly drives toward the

No Star Power

During the Bulls' first 32 seasons, from 1966 to 1998, they had at least one player make the All-Star team 29 times. The 1975, 1980, and 1984 All-Star Games were the only ones that did not feature a Bull. After the breakup of the 1998 championship team, the Bulls went 11 straight years without an All-Star, from 1999 to 2009. Derrick Rose ended that streak when he was selected for the 2010 All-Star Game.

basket, and his acrobatic layups. After the 2010–11 regular season, Rose became the youngest league MVP ever at 22 years old.

In the 13 seasons after the Bulls won the 1998 NBA title, they had nine different head coaches. Tom Thibodeau became the coach prior to the 2010–11 season. Thibodeau placed a heavy emphasis on defense, and throughout the season the team did not lose more than two games in a row.

SELECT COMPANY

Derrick Rose was named the NBA's Rookie of the Year in 2008–09. He became the third Bull to win the award. Michael Jordan had won it in 1984–85, and Elton Brand had won the award in 1999–2000.

Rose was born in Englewood, one of Chicago's rougher neighborhoods. Knowing his dream to bring an NBA title back to Chicago, his three older brothers coached him through a star-studded high school career. After just one year of college, the Bulls selected him with the first overall pick of the 2008 draft. He knew all about the team's great history and the standard that Michael Jordan had set for Chicago.

"I would love to be that guy," Rose said. "To be behind Mike, or even get close to him, the way I look at it, would be great. People will remember you. That's what I want people to remember about me: that I gave my all, and I was a winner."

Prior to the 2010–11 season, Chicago added veteran big man Carlos Boozer. With Rose leading the way and Boozer, Deng, and Joakim Noah by his side, the Bulls immediately proved to be one of the most talented teams in the Eastern Conference.

The Bulls had surprised everyone with a 62–20 record heading into the 2011 playoffs. They wowed fans and critics alike with their lockdown defense and their unselfish passing. However, the road ahead would not be easy. In the first series, Chicago won four hard-fought games to oust the rival Indiana Pacers from postseason play. They gave up two games to the Atlanta Hawks in the second series. By the time they faced the Miami Heat in the Eastern Conference finals, they seemed to have hit their stride. They

The Bulls' Carlos Boozer, *right*, lays off a pass to Joakim Noah, *left*, despite pressure from the Toronto Raptors on February 23, 2011.

easily defeated LeBron James and Dwyane Wade's much-hyped team 103–82 in Game 1.

The Bulls' playoff run would not have its fairytale ending, though. The Heat did not lose another game. They defeated Chicago 4–1 to win the Eastern Conference and move on to the NBA Finals. Chicago fans were devastated. But with the youngest-ever MVP and the Coach of the Year at the helm, the team's future was as bright as ever.

TIMELINE

1966	The Chicago Bulls are formed and become the 10th team in the NBA.
1974	Under the direction of coach Dick Motta, the Bulls reach the Western Conference finals for the first time in team history. The next season, they again make it to the conference finals.
1984	With the number three overall pick in the NBA Draft, the Bulls draft University of North Carolina star Michael Jordan.
1985	Led by Jordan, who was named NBA Rookie of the Year, the Bulls make the playoffs for the first time in four years. It was the first of 14 straight playoff appearances.
1988	Jordan wins the first of his five NBA MVP Awards.
1989	Phil Jackson is named head coach of the Bulls.
1991	Jackson, Jordan, and Scottie Pippen lead the Bulls to their first NBA championship. They beat the Los Angeles Lakers four games to one. Jordan is named the MVP of both the league and the Finals.
1992	The Bulls go 67–15 during the regular season and win a second consecutive NBA championship. Once again, Jordan is named MVP for the regular season and the NBA Finals.
1993	For a third straight season, the Bulls win the NBA championship. They beat the Phoenix Suns four games to two.

| 1995 | Jordan returns to the Bulls after a 21-month retirement. However, he cannot lead the Bulls back to another NBA title. They lose to the Orlando Magic in the second round. |

| 1996 | Jordan, Pippen, Dennis Rodman, and Jackson lead the Bulls to an NBA-record 72 wins during the regular season. They cruise through the playoffs to win their fourth NBA title in six years. |

| 1997 | After a 69-win season, the Bulls win another NBA championship. They beat the Utah Jazz four games to two. |

| 1998 | Jordan wins the MVP Award for the fifth time and leads the Bulls to their sixth NBA championship in eight years. After the NBA Finals, Jordan, Pippen, Jackson, and Rodman leave the team. |

| 2000 | Elton Brand, who had been the first draft pick in 1999, becomes the second Bull to win NBA Rookie of the Year honors. |

| 2005 | For the first time in seven years, the Bulls return to the NBA playoffs. |

| 2008 | The Bulls draft University of Memphis star Derrick Rose with the first pick in the NBA Draft. He wins the NBA Rookie of the Year Award. |

| 2011 | Derrick Rose becomes the youngest MVP in league history, and Tom Thibodeau is named Coach of the Year. The Bulls finish the regular season with the best record, 62–20, but are knocked out of the playoffs by the Miami Heat in the Eastern Conference finals. |

QUICK STATS

FRANCHISE HISTORY
Chicago Bulls (1966–)

NBA FINALS
(1966– ; wins in bold)
1991, 1992, 1993, 1996, 1997, 1998

CONFERENCE CHAMPIONSHIPS
1991, 1992, 1993, 1996, 1997, 1998

DIVISION CHAMPIONSHIPS
1975, 1992, 1993, 1996, 1997, 1998, 2011

KEY PLAYERS
(position[s]; seasons with team)
Artis Gilmore (C; 1976–82, 1987)
Horace Grant (F/C; 1987–94)

Michael Jordan (G/F; 1984–93, 1995–98)
Bob Love (F; 1968–77)
John Paxson (G; 1985–94)
Scottie Pippen (F/G; 1987–98; 2003–04)
Dennis Rodman (F; 1995–98)
Derrick Rose (G; 2008–)
Jerry Sloan (G; 1966–76)
Reggie Theus (G; 1978–84)
Norm Van Lier (G; 1971–78)
Chet Walker (F; 1969–75)

KEY COACHES
Doug Collins (1986–89): 137–109; 13–17 (postseason)
Phil Jackson (1989–98): 545–193; 111–41 (postseason)
Dick Motta (1968–76): 356–300; 18–29 (postseason)

HOME ARENAS
International Amphitheatre (1966–67)
Chicago Stadium (1967–94)
United Center (1994–)

* All statistics through 2010–11 season

QUOTES AND ANECDOTES

Bob Cousy is a Hall of Famer and one of the greatest Boston Celtics of all time. He was very close to gaining his stardom in Chicago, however. In 1950, the Chicago Stags bought Cousy's rights from the Tri-Cities Blackhawks. But the Stags folded before Cousy ever played for them. The Celtics then picked him up, and he became a 13-time All-Star and a six-time NBA champion.

Dick Motta was one of the best coaches in Bulls history. Unlike another great Bulls coach, Phil Jackson, Motta did not have NBA playing experience. In fact, Motta never played varsity basketball in high school, and he did not play at Utah State, where he went to college. He got his start in coaching at Grace Junior High School in Utah when he was just 23 years old.

Heading into the 2010–11 season, Jerry Sloan, Phil Jackson, and Dick Motta all ranked among the top 10 winningest coaches in NBA history. All three of them got their first NBA head coaching jobs with the Bulls.

During the Bulls' first season in 1966–67, Guy Rodgers set an NBA record with 908 assists. That record has since been broken several times, but Rodgers still held the Bulls' record as of 2010–11.

"He was perhaps the most recognizable athlete in the world for a decade . . . That he brought the game of basketball and the NBA to that level will never be eclipsed." — Phil Jackson on Michael Jordan when he was inducted into the players' Hall of Fame in 2009

GLOSSARY

archrival

The opponent that brings out the greatest emotion in a team, its fans, and its players.

assist

A pass that leads directly to a made basket.

backcourt

The point guards and shooting guards on a basketball team.

broadcaster

An announcer who describes or talks about sporting events on television or radio.

contract

A binding agreement about, for example, years of commitment by a basketball player in exchange for a given salary.

draft

A system used by professional sports leagues to select new players in order to spread incoming talent among all teams. The NBA Draft is held each June.

expansion

In sports, the addition of a franchise or franchises to a league.

general manager

The executive who is in charge of the team's overall operation. He or she hires and fires coaches, drafts players, and signs free agents.

lockout

When an employer prevents employees from working, usually due to a labor dispute.

postseason

The games in which the best teams play after the regular-season schedule has been completed.

rebound

To secure the basketball after a missed shot.

rookie

A first-year player in the NBA.

roster

The players as a whole on a basketball team.

FOR MORE INFORMATION

Further Reading

Christopher, Matt, and Glenn Stout. *Michael Jordan: Legends in Sports.* New York: Little Brown Books for Young Readers, 2008.

Levine, David. *The Chicago Bulls: The Best Ever.* New York: Time, 1997.

Wong, Adam. *Derrick Rose.* San Diego, CA: Lucent Books, 2010.

Web Links

To learn more about the Chicago Bulls, visit ABDO Publishing Company online at **www.abdopublishing.com**. Web sites about the Bulls are featured on our Book Links page. These links are routinely monitored and updated to provide the most current information available.

Places To Visit

Chicagoland Sports Hall of Fame
3501 S. Laramie
Stickney-Cicero, IL 60804
708-780-3700
www.chicagolandsportshalloffame.com
This memorial to Chicago sports greats is located at the Hawthorne Race Course in Cicero, Illinois. Bulls players such as Bob Love, John Paxson, and George Wilson are honored here.

Naismith Memorial Basketball Hall of Fame
1000 West Columbus Avenue
Springfield, MA 01105-2518
413-781-6500
www.hoophall.com
This Hall of Fame and museum highlights the greatest players and moments in the history of basketball. Former Bulls players Michael Jordan and Scottie Pippen are among the inductees.

United Center
1901 West Madison Street
Chicago, IL 60612
312-455-4500
www.unitedcenter.com
This is the home arena for the Chicago Bulls. They play 41 home games here each season.

INDEX

About the Author

Brian Howell is a freelance writer based in Denver, Colorado. He has published several books for youth and has been a sports journalist for more than 17 years. During that time he has written about high school, college, and professional athletics, including major sporting events such as the U.S. Open golf tournament, the World Series, the Stanley Cup playoffs, the NBA All-Star Game, and the NBA playoffs. He has earned several writing awards throughout his career. He lives with his wife and four children in Colorado.

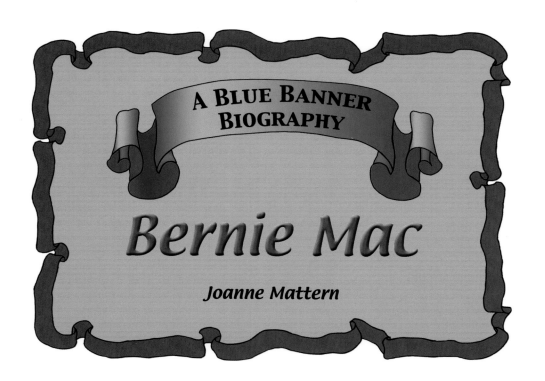

A BLUE BANNER BIOGRAPHY

Bernie Mac

Joanne Mattern

Mitchell Lane
PUBLISHERS

P.O. Box 196
Hockessin, Delaware 19707
Visit us on the web: www.mitchelllane.com
Comments? email us: mitchelllane@mitchelllane.com

Mitchell Lane PUBLISHERS

Printing   2   3   4   5   6   7   8   9

Blue Banner Biographies

Alan Jackson	Alicia Keys	Allen Iverson
Ashanti	Ashlee Simpson	Ashton Kutcher
Avril Lavigne	**Bernie Mac**	Beyoncé
Bow Wow	Britney Spears	Christina Aguilera
Christopher Paul Curtis	Clay Aiken	Condoleezza Rice
Daniel Radcliffe	Derek Jeter	Eminem
Eve	50 Cent	Gwen Stefani
Ice Cube	Jamie Foxx	Ja Rule
Jay-Z	Jennifer Lopez	J. K. Rowling
Jodie Foster	Justin Berfield	Kate Hudson
Kelly Clarkson	Kenny Chesney	Lance Armstrong
Lindsay Lohan	Mariah Carey	Mario
Mary-Kate and Ashley Olsen	Melissa Gilbert	Michael Jackson
Miguel Tejada	Missy Elliott	Nelly
Orlando Bloom	P. Diddy	Paris Hilton
Peyton Manning	Queen Latifah	Rita Williams-Garcia
Ritchie Valens	Ron Howard	Rudy Giuliani
Sally Field	Selena	Shirley Temple
Tim McGraw	Usher	

Library of Congress Cataloging-in-Publication Data
Mattern, Joanne, 1963–
    Bernie Mac/ by Joanne Mattern.
          p. cm. — (Blue banner biographies)
    Includes bibliographical references and index.
    ISBN 1-58415-488-8 (library bound: alk. paper)
    1. Mac, Bernie—Juvenile literature. 2. Actors—United States—Biography—Juvenile
literature. 3. Comedians—United States—Biography—Juvenile literature.
    I. Title. II. Series: Blue banner biography.
    PN2287.M166M38 2006
    792. 702'8092—dc22
    [B]
                                                2006014805

ISBN-10: 1-58415-488-8   ISBN-13: 9781584154884

ABOUT THE AUTHOR: Joanne Mattern is the author of more than 100 nonfiction books for children, including *Peyton Manning* and *Miguel Tejada* for Mitchell Lane Publishers. Along with biographies, she has written extensively about animals, nature, history, sports, and foreign cultures. She lives near New York City with her husband and three young daughters.

PHOTO CREDITS: Cover and p. 4: Globe Photos; p. 8 Getty Images; p. 10 Mychal Watts WireImage.com; p. 14 Frederick M. Brown/Getty Images; p. 18 Scott Gries/Getty Images; pp. 23, 26 Globe Photos; p. 28 Gregg DeGuire/WireImage.com

CONTENTS

Bernie Mac poses for his television series, The Bernie Mac Show. *The show made Bernie one of today's most successful comedians.*

A Tough Crowd

*B*ernie Mac stood backstage, waiting to perform his comedy routine. The show would be taped as part of Def Comedy Jam, which would air on the cable-TV channel HBO.

As Bernie waited, he watched another comedian onstage. The comedian was not doing well. The crowd booed and yelled at him. Finally, the comedian walked off in defeat.

Def Comedy Jam's host, a comedian named Martin Lawrence, tried to get the crowd to calm down. His efforts just made the crowd angrier. Lawrence could not control them. Finally, he motioned for Bernie Mac to come on. Lawrence walked off the stage without even introducing him.

Bernie Mac had played in a lot of comedy clubs, and he had played to a lot of tough crowds. He knew he had to work hard and fast to get the audience on his side. In spite of the pressure, Bernie felt good. "I wasn't nervous," he said later, "because I knew they wanted to see me fail. I work better when things are against me, when people don't believe in me. It ignites me."

Def Comedy Jam was one of the first big breaks in Bernie Mac's career.

Bernie walked onto the stage, picked up the microphone, and looked out over the audience. Then he yelled, "I ain't scared of you!" The crowd cheered. Bernie started telling jokes. Everyone laughed. They cheered. Bernie did a great comedy routine. The audience loved him!

Def Comedy Jam was one of the first big breaks in Bernie Mac's career. He went on to star in movies, had a successful TV show, and played in comedy clubs all over the country.

Bernie Mac's life was not always so wonderful. He came from a very poor family and had many troubles while he was growing up. Bernie never let himself quit, and he always worked hard to overcome his problems. Here is the story of a boy who grew up to make millions of people laugh.

Growing Up Poor

*B*ernard Jeffrey McCullough was born in Chicago, Illinois, on October 5, 1957. His father left the family when Bernie was a little boy. Bernie and his brother Darryl lived with their mother, Mary McCullough. Darryl was about ten years older than Bernie. The family also included Bernie's grandparents and other relatives. Bernie's mother worked as a supervisor in a hospital.

The big family crowded into a tiny house. When Bernie was little, the house was torn down because the city said the neighborhood was not safe. The McCulloughs moved to an apartment above the Burning Bush Baptist Church. Bernie's grandfather was a deacon in the church.

The McCulloughs were very poor. Bernie remembers days when there was nothing to eat in the refrigerator

Bernie talks to host Jay Leno on The Tonight Show *in 2003. Bernie has come a long way from the difficult days of his childhood.*

except a few slices of bologna and some beans. The best day of the week was Sunday. "Sundays we had a real dinner," Bernie wrote in his autobiography, *Maybe You Never Cry Again.* "Roast and mashed potatoes and butter rolls and macaroni and cheese and gravy, boatloads of gravy. That was some serious eating. I couldn't wait for Sundays."

Bernie was a small boy, but he had very big eyes. People called him Spooky Juice because his big, bright eyes made him look scary.

Bernie's mother and grandparents were very strict. There were a lot of rules in the McCullough house. If Bernie broke a rule, his mother and grandparents would yell at him and sometimes hit him. His mother would tell him, "I know you don't like it, and I know you're mad at me. But life isn't a popularity contest." Bernie learned to respect adults.

Although she was strict, Bernie loved his mother very much. She called him Beanie. She believed in him more than anyone else. "Don't you worry about Beanie. Beanie gonna be just fine," she would say.

One night, when Bernie was about four years old, he saw his mother crying in front of the television. He climbed into her lap and tried to wipe away her tears with his fingers. More than anything, he wanted to make those tears stop.

A comedian named Bill Cosby came on the television and started telling jokes. Suddenly, Bernie's mother stopped crying and started laughing. Soon she was laughing so hard, she was shaking. Bernie was amazed. He realized that telling jokes could be a powerful thing.

> *Although she was strict, Bernie loved his mother very much. She called him Beanie. She believed in him more than anyone.*

"That's what I want to be, Mama," Bernie said. "A comedian. Make you laugh like that, maybe you never cry again."

Bernie practiced being funny. He told jokes at school. Sometimes his joke-telling got him into trouble. Other times, his teachers would ask him to stand in front of the

In 2003, Bernie published his autobiography, Maybe You Never Cry Again. *The book describes Bernie's difficult childhood and his determination to succeed as a comedian.*

room and tell stories. When he was alone, Bernie told jokes to himself. He was always trying to be funny.

When he was about eight years old, someone at church asked him to tell his funny stories during services. Bernie talked about his grandparents. He made fun of the way his grandfather said everything four times. Soon everyone in the church was laughing—even his grandparents!

As Bernie got older, life got harder. Many of his friends got in trouble with drugs, while other young men in his neighborhood joined gangs. Drugs and gangs seemed glamorous and were big temptations, but Bernie stayed away from them. He knew the truth: that drugs and gangs were dangerous and could ruin his life.

His family also made sure Bernie stayed safe by creating more rules for him. They would not let him hang around in the park after dark, and they made sure he came home for dinner every night. Bernie did not always like their rules, but he knew that his family loved him. They wanted the best for him.

Drugs and gangs seemed glamorous. Bernie knew the truth: that drugs and gangs could ruin his life.

Sad Times

When Bernie was fifteen years old, his mother asked him to come with her to visit someone. She took him to a nice neighborhood in Chicago, and they stopped in front of a house with a yard. Bernie had never seen such a nice-looking home in his life.

Then Bernie got a big surprise. His mother told him the house was theirs. She had bought it with the money she had earned working overtime at the hospital.

Bernie and his family were very happy to move into the new house. "We felt rich," Bernie wrote later.

Darryl was on his own by this time, so Mary McCullough gave all her attention to Bernie. To make sure he had a good education, she made him take a test so that he could get into Chicago Vocational High School. This school had a better reputation than the regular high school in Bernie's new neighborhood.

Life was going well for Bernie, but all that was about to change. For a long time, Bernie's mother had been sick. Bernie knew something was wrong, but his family would not talk about it. Finally, his mother was too sick to hide it anymore. She had cancer. In August 1974, when Bernie was not quite sixteen years old, Mary McCullough died.

After his mother died, Bernie continued to live with his grandparents. His aunt Evelyn lived with the family and helped take care of Bernie, too.

A year after Bernie's mother died, his uncle came to get him at school. He had bad news for Bernie. Darryl had died of a heart attack. He was only twenty-seven years old.

Because Darryl was ten years older than Bernie, the two had not spent much time together. Despite their age difference, Bernie admired his older brother and

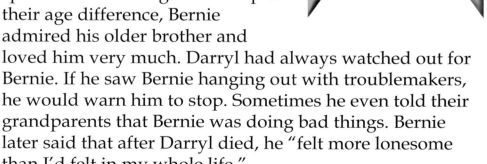

In August 1974, when Bernie was not quite sixteen years old, his mother, Mary McCullough, died.

loved him very much. Darryl had always watched out for Bernie. If he saw Bernie hanging out with troublemakers, he would warn him to stop. Sometimes he even told their grandparents that Bernie was doing bad things. Bernie later said that after Darryl died, he "felt more lonesome than I'd felt in my whole life."

Bernie and his wife, Rhonda, attend the 35th Annual NAACP Image Awards in 2004. Bernie and Rhonda were high school sweethearts. They have been married since 1977.

Life went on for the McCullough family. Bernie began to pay more attention in school. He had never taken his studies very seriously before, but once he did, he discovered he liked school. His best subjects were English and history. A lot of his friends made fun of him. They thought studying was a waste of time. Bernie didn't agree. "I'm beginning to figure it out," Bernie wrote. "You're not smart, you're going nowhere fast. So get smart, brother."

Bernie graduated from high school in 1975. That year, a new television show came on called *Saturday Night Live*. The show featured outrageous comedy sketches performed live. Bernie loved the show. He had always enjoyed telling jokes. Now he wondered if he could be a comedian just like the people he saw on TV. It was a big dream. Bernie would have to work hard to make that dream come true.

> *Bernie had never taken his studies very seriously before, but once he did, he discovered he liked school.*

A Big Change

For several years, Bernie had been going out with a girl named Rhonda. In 1977, Rhonda told him she was going to have a baby. Bernie was very excited. Many young men in the same situation do not want to take the responsibility of raising a family. Bernie felt differently. Bernie loved Rhonda, and he wanted to spend his life with her. The two got married on September 17, 1977. A few months later, Rhonda gave birth to their daughter. They named her Je'Niece.

Bernie took any job he could find to take care of his family. At different times, he worked as a janitor at a General Motors car factory, drove delivery trucks, and fried fish at a fast-food restaurant. Rhonda worked as a nurse. Even with both Rhonda and Bernie working, the family was barely able to pay all their bills.

Bernie had not given up his dream of being a comedian. He often told jokes on the subway when he was going to and from work. Sometimes people gave him money. Later, he performed at parties and dances and began to appear at small clubs around Chicago.

Bernie told jokes about his life. He talked about his grandparents, his mother, his wife, and their friends. Bernie liked to "tell it like it is," and people responded well to his jokes. They recognized themselves in the people and events Bernie joked about.

During the early 1980s, Bernie and his family took a short vacation to Las Vegas. They went to see a show by Redd Foxx, a legendary African-American comedian. Before the show, Bernie was walking around the theater. He spotted Redd Foxx in his dressing room and went in to say hello. Bernie told Foxx he was a comedian. To his surprise, Foxx asked him if he wanted to perform for five minutes at the beginning of the show. Bernie said yes!

Redd Foxx asked Bernie if he wanted to perform at the beginning of his show. Bernie said yes!

Bernie went onstage and began to "tell it like it is." He joked about his relationship with his wife and his family. The crowd laughed so hard that Foxx let Bernie do his routine for a lot longer than just five minutes.

After Bernie came offstage, Foxx gave him advice. "You're funny," the older man said. "But you do have one little problem. You're funny, but you don't want to be funny. You want to be liked. Now if you open yourself up, and you get real, and you start taking comedy seriously — well, there's no telling how far you'll go. You're afraid to show people what you've got inside. And that's where the best stuff is."

Foxx also told Bernie not to be afraid to fail. Bernie listened. He respected Redd Foxx and knew the man had given him excellent advice. From then on, Bernie did not hold anything back. He was even more determined to be a comedian.

Bernie appears on MTV's Total Request Live *in 2004.* The Bernie Mac Show *and his movie appearances have made Bernie very popular among young people.*

Slowly, Bernie's dream started to come true. He appeared regularly at a big Chicago theater called the Cotton Club. In 1990, someone from the Cotton Club entered Bernie in a contest called the Miller Lite Comedy Search. One hundred comedians performed in clubs and theaters all over Chicago. A group of judges narrowed the field down to the top ten. Bernie was one of them!

The final show was held at the Regal Theater in Chicago. The host was Damon Wayans, a popular young comedian. Bernie did such a great act that he won the contest.

Bernie's career took off. He was invited to perform all over the United States. During the weekdays, he drove a Wonder Bread delivery truck. Every weekend, he traveled around the country doing comedy.

It was time for Bernie to make a decision. Did he want the safety of having a regular job? Or did he want to take a risk and work as a comedian? Bernie decided to take the risk. Just before Thanksgiving in 1991, he quit his job. He was going to be a full-time comedian.

Did he want the safety of a regular job? Or did he want to take a risk and work as a comedian? Bernie decided to take the risk.

Rhonda was shocked when he told her he had quit his job. In spite of her surprise, she was not angry. She knew that being a comedian was what Bernie really wanted to do. Rhonda supported his decision. Bernie started his new life knowing that his wife was behind him all the way.

Success!

*B*ernie did not waste any time moving his career to the next level. He appeared in two Def Comedy Jam specials on HBO.

One day in 1991, Damon Wayans called. Bernie had not seen Wayans since the Miller Lite Comedy Search. Wayans had gone on to have a popular television show called *In Living Color.* Now he was making a movie called *Mo' Money.* He offered Bernie a small part in the movie. Bernie said yes.

Bernie also appeared on television. In 1993 he took part in an HBO comedy special called *Rosie Perez Presents Society's Ride.* He also hosted his own comedy and musical show at the Cotton Club in Chicago and continued to appear in comedy clubs and theaters all over the country.

Then Bernie got to appear in another movie. A director named Ted Demme called and offered him the part of a barber in his movie *Who's the Man?* Bernie had a good time making the movie, and he and Ted Demme became close friends.

Bernie went on to appear in other comedies—*House Party 3* and *Above the Rim.* Later, he had a chance to play a serious role. In *The Walking Dead,* he played a soldier.

Bernie did not have big roles in those movies. Still, the parts meant a lot to him. "Every moment in front of the cameras was a chance to learn something new," he wrote in *Maybe You Never Cry Again.* "And that's what I was doing: I was keeping my eyes and ears open and learning."

Bernie appeared in a lot of movies in the late 1990s. He also had his own show on HBO, called *Midnight Mac.* Bernie was proud of the show, but the network canceled it after just one month because it was not getting great ratings.

> *Bernie had more success with his role on the TV show Moesha, which starred singer Brandy Norwood.*

Bernie had more success with his role on the TV show *Moesha,* which starred the talented singer Brandy Norwood as a teenage girl. Moesha was a groundbreaking show, because it was the first situation comedy to center around an African-American girl. The show also won praise for the way it dealt responsibly with controversial issues instead of using these situations just to make jokes, as other comedies did.

Still, many people did not know who Bernie Mac was. Soon, a movie would change all that.

In 1998, Bernie appeared in *The Kings of Comedy,* a show that featured three African-American comedians: Steve Harvey, Cedric Kyles (who is called Cedric the Entertainer), and Bernie Mac. In 1999, another comedian, D.L. Hughley, joined the show.

The Kings of Comedy toured all over the country and became the most popular comedy act in America. Almost all of the audiences were black. One reporter called the show "The Biggest Show Business Phenomenon Most White People Didn't Even Know About."

In 2000, director Spike Lee filmed several shows on the tour and made a movie called *The Original Kings of Comedy.* The movie was very popular with both black and white audiences. Finally, white America got to know Bernie Mac.

The Original Kings of Comedy movie was very popular. Finally, white America got to know Bernie Mac.

During *The Kings of Comedy,* Bernie Mac did a very funny routine. He said that he was raising his two young nieces and a nephew because his sister had a drug problem and couldn't take care of them. The children were a handful, and Bernie threatened to do all sorts of damage to them in the name of tough love. The story was based on

The cast of the Bernie Mac Show (left to right): Jeremy Suarez, Kellita Smith, Camille Winbush (front), Bernie Mac, and Dee Dee Davis. The TV series is based on the experiences of one of Bernie's friends.

the experiences of a friend who was raising his sister's children. The crowd loved Bernie's stories.

Television producers loved his stories too. Bernie went to Los Angeles to meet a writer named Larry Wilmore. He and Wilmore came up with the idea of a television show based on Bernie's comedy routine about raising his nieces and nephew.

The very popular *Bernie Mac Show* went on the air in 2001. Bernie insisted that the character remain true to the character in his comedy shows. He also insisted that the relationship between his character and his character's wife be a good one. He wanted viewers to see a strong, happy marriage in which both partners were equals—the sort of marriage Bernie and Rhonda had. Although they fought sometimes, they loved and respected each other.

Bernie also wanted the show to be realistic in other ways. The show did not use a laugh track, and Bernie often spoke directly to the television audience. Despite the very funny things that happened on the show, Bernie also insisted that it portray racial and religious situations seriously and respectfully.

> *Bernie also insisted that the show portray racial and religious situations seriously and respectfully.*

Bernie also appeared in more movies, and now he was landing bigger roles. He played a blackjack dealer in the comedies *Ocean's Eleven* and *Ocean's Twelve.* These movies featured all-star casts, including George Clooney, Matt Damon, Brad Pitt, and Julia Roberts, and were a huge success with audiences.

In 2002, Bernie Mac stopped appearing in comedy clubs. He felt that, at age forty-five, he was too old to do so many shows a week. Instead, he concentrated on making himself a star of movies and television.

In 2004, Bernie finally had his first starring role—as a baseball player trying to make a comeback in *Mr. 3000.* Bernie picked that movie because it wasn't all outrageous comedy. He wanted to show people he could also be a serious actor. "People will see me in a whole different light," Bernie promised a reporter for *Entertainment Weekly* in 2004. "I love making people say, 'I didn't know he could do that.'"

Bernie also had major roles in *Bad Santa* and *Charlie's Angels: Full Throttle.* In 2005, he starred in *Guess Who.* That film was a remake of a 1967 classic movie called *Guess Who's Coming to Dinner?* about a marriage between a white girl and a black man. In the remake, the roles were reversed. Bernie played the father in an African-American family who was upset that his daughter was marrying a white man, played by Ashton Kutcher. Bernie enjoyed the comedy aspects of the movie, and also felt it sent a strong message about tolerance.

Bernie revealed he had been suffering from a disease called sarcoidosis for more than twenty years.

Everything seemed to be going well for Bernie, but in 2005, he suffered a health scare. After he finished making *Ocean's Twelve,* he was hospitalized with pneumonia. When he recovered, Bernie revealed that he had been suffering from a disease called sarcoidosis for more than twenty years. This rare but very serious disease causes inflammation of the body's tissues and often affects the lungs.

"I've had sarcoidosis since 1983, and it has not altered or limited my lifestyle," Bernie told *Star* magazine. "No one knows where sarcoidosis comes from or where it starts, and there's no known cure for this condition that affects primarily minorities." He went on to say that sarcoidosis had not slowed him down and that he was still able to "play basketball and do normal things." Bernie added, "Since sarcoidosis hasn't slowed me down, then it shouldn't be a concern for others." He planned to raise public awareness of the disease and start a foundation to help others with the condition.

In 2006, Bernie Mac's television show was in its fifth successful season. He was also continuing to make movies. He costarred in *P.D.R.*, a movie that tells the true story of Jim Ellis, a Philadelphia man who started a swim team for troubled black teenagers during the 1970s and made them champions. The year also saw Bernie filming *Ocean's*

Bernie and Ashton Kutcher starred in the movie Guess Who *in 2005. The comedy focused on a black family learning to accept their white son-in-law.*

Thirteen, the third in a successful series of movies about a gang of high-stakes thieves.

Bernie enjoys making movies, but he never watches himself on screen. "I don't watch myself because it makes me uncomfortable," he told a reporter from *Essence* magazine in 2003. He also said he does not feel the need to study himself on film. "When I act, I do things from my heart so much that it drains me. I don't need to go back because I gave you all I can. I gave you my best."

Bernie has become a very wealthy man. He knows that being rich and famous gives him a responsibility to help others. However, he does not always give to major charities. "I don't like to be told where to give," he wrote. "I don't like to be told what I need to do for the community. I like to give for many different reasons. I do it because I believe in that donation. I believe it's going to help people."

Bernie has supported members of his family when they were in financial difficulties. He also helps his friends. When a close friend died, Bernie made sure the man's children were taken care of financially.

> **Bernie has supported family and friends. When a close friend died, Bernie made sure the man's children were taken care of.**

Bernie's first priority has always been his family. He and Rhonda have been married since 1977 and have a strong, happy marriage. Je'Niece is married and going to

Bernie appears with his wife, Rhonda (right); his daughter, Je'Niece; and his son-in-law, Trey Childress, at the premiere of Mr. 3000 *in 2004. Bernie is very proud of his family.*

school. Bernie is very proud that his daughter has grown up into a smart, confident, and beautiful young woman.

As a role model, Bernie always tries to set a good example for young people. He talks about the importance of tough love. He encourages students to stay in school and stay away from drugs. His own life is an example that working hard can make you a big success.

Bernie Mac has made a living at being funny. Yet this comedian takes comedy very seriously. "I always want to top myself. I want to get good," he told a reporter from *Time Canada* magazine. "I want the audience to leave the theater and say, 'He did good.'"

"Doing good" is something Bernie Mac definitely has accomplished!

CHRONOLOGY

1957 Bernard Jeffrey McCullough is born in Chicago, Illinois, on October 5.

1974 Bernie's mother dies of cancer.

1975 Bernie's brother dies of a heart attack; Bernie graduates from Chicago Vocational High School.

1977 Bernie marries his high school sweetheart, Rhonda, on September 17.

1978 Bernie and Rhonda's daughter, Je'Niece, is born.

1990 Bernie wins the Miller Lite Comedy Search.

1991 Bernie quits his job to be a comedian full-time.

1992 Bernie appears in his first movie, *Mo' Money.*

1998 Bernie tours with *The Kings of Comedy.*

2000 *The Original Kings of Comedy* becomes a popular movie.

2001 *The Bernie Mac Show* goes on the air; Bernie publishes *I Ain't Scared of You;* he appears in *Ocean's Eleven.*

2003 Bernie publishes his autobiography, *Maybe You Never Cry Again.*

2004 Bernie stars in *Mr. 3000* and costars in *Ocean's Twelve.*

2005 Bernie reveals he has sarcoidosis; he stars in *Guess Who; The Bernie Mac Show* wins numerous awards, including the prestigious Peabody and Humanitas Awards, an Emmy Award for Outstanding Writing for a Comedy Series, and three NAACP Image Awards for Outstanding Comedy Series.

2006 Bernie costars in *P.D.R.* and *Ocean's Thirteen.*

FILMOGRAPHY

1992	*Mo' Money*
1993	*Who's the Man?*
1994	*House Party 3*
	Above the Rim
1995	*The Walking Dead*
	Friday
1996	*Reasons*
	Don't Be a Menace to South Central While Drinking Your Juice in the Hood
	Get on the Bus
1997	*Booty Call*
	B*A*P*S
	How to Be a Player
1998	*The Players Club*
2000	*The Original Kings of Comedy*
2001	*What's the Worst That Could Happen?*
	Ocean's Eleven
2003	*Head of State*
	Charlie's Angels: Full Throttle
	Bad Santa
2004	*Mr. 3000*
	Ocean's Twelve
2005	*Guess Who*
2007	*Ocean's Thirteen*

FURTHER READING

Magazines

Boscia, Ted. "Bernie Mac," *Scholastic Action,* March 28, 2003, Volume
  26, Issue 12, pp. 4–5.
"In the Spotlight: Bernie Mac," *Biography,* July 2003, Volume 7, Issue 7,
  p. 14.

On the Internet

ACESHOWBIZ:Bernie Mac
  http://www.aceshowbiz.com/celebrity/bernie_mac/
Internet Movie Database: Bernie Mac
  http://www.imdb.com/name/nm0005170/
People: Bernie Mac
  http://people.aol.com/people/searchresults?search=Bernie+Mac
UPN57: "The Bernie Mac Show."
  http://upn57.com/upn57shows/local_story_265142817.html

Works Consulted
Books

Mac, Bernie, with Darrell Dawsey. *I Ain't Scared of You.* New York:
  Pocket Books, 2001.
Mac, Bernie. *Maybe You Never Cry Again.* New York: HarperCollins, 2003.

Magazines

Amber, Jeannine. "The Mix," *Essence,* June 2003, Volume 34, Issue 2,
  pp. 218–223.
Binelli, Mark. "Bernie Mac's Hostile Takeover," *Rolling Stone,*
  December 26, 2003, Issue 912–913, pp. 39–40.
Kirschling, Gregory. "Big MAC Attack," *Entertainment Weekly,*
  September 24, 2004, Issue 785, pp. 40–41.
Winters, Rebecca. "Q & A With Bernie Mac," *Time Canada,* December
  1, 2003, Vol. 162, Issue 22, p. 79.

INDEX